Workbook

American Headway 2A

John and Liz Soars

OXFORD
UNIVERSITY PRESS

198 Madison Avenue
New York, NY 10016 USA

Great Clarendon Street
Oxford OX2 6DP England

Oxford New York

Auckland Cape Town Dar es Salaam Hong Kong Karachi
Kuala Lumpur Madrid Melbourne Mexico City Nairobi
New Delhi Shanghai Taipei Toronto

With offices in

Argentina Austria Brazil Chile Czech Republic France Greece
Guatemala Hungary Italy Japan Poland Portugal Singapore
South Korea Switzerland Thailand Turkey Ukraine Vietnam

OXFORD is a trademark of Oxford University Press.

ISBN: 978 0 19 438906 8

Copyright © 2004 Oxford University Press

No unauthorized photocopying.

All rights reserved. No part of this publication may be reproduced, stored in a retrieval system, or transmitted, in any form or by any means, electronic, mechanical, photocopying, recording, or otherwise, without the prior written permission of Oxford University Press.

This book is sold subject to the condition that it shall not, by way of trade or otherwise, be lent, resold, hired out, or otherwise circulated without the publisher's prior consent in any form of binding or cover other than that in which it is published and without a similar condition including this condition being imposed on the subsequent purchaser.

American Headway Workbook 2A:
Editorial Manager: Jeff krum
Editor/Page Layout: Tünde A. Dewey
Art Director: Lynn Luchetti
Production Manager: Shanta Persaud
Production Assistant: Zainaltu Jawat Ali

Printing (last digit): 10 9 8 7

Printed in China.

Acknowledgments

Cover concept: Rowie Christopher
Cover design: Rowie Christopher and Silver Editions

Illustrations by
Adrian Barclay, John Batten, Kathy Baxendale,
Emma Dodd/Black Hat, Mark Duffin, Neil Gower,
Tim Kahane, Zina Saunders, Harry Venning, Celia Witchard

Handwriting and realia by
Kathy Baxendale

Location and studio photography by
Phillip Dunn, Mark Mason, Tony Ward/Metcalfe

The publisher would like to thank the following for their permission to reproduce photographs:
R Adams/Telegraph Colour Library; Alaska Stock; D. Armand/Stone; B. Aron/Stone; Aviation Picture Library; Bruce Ayers/Stone; Tore Bergsaker/Sygma; The BettmannArchive/Corbis; The Boulder Colorado Chamber of Commerce; Jason Childs/FPG; P. Choiniere/Stone; Comnet Ltd./Telegraph Colour Library; Corbis UK Ltd; P. Correz/Stone; Mark Crosse/AP Worldwide; George B. Diebold/The Stockmarket; G. Du Feu/Bubbles Photolibrary; D. Durfee/Stone; Jillian Edelstein/Sygma; R. Frerck/Stone; Tony Gervis/Robert Harding Picture Library; S. Godlewski/Stone; Michael Goldman/FPG; Blaine Harrington/The Stock Market; Mark Heifner/Panoramic Images; C. Henderson/Stone; John Henley/The Stockmarket; W. Hodges/Stone; Michael Keller/The Stockmarket; C. Kunin/Stone; R. Leeney/Telegraph Colour Library; Lightscapes Inc./The Stockmarket; R. Mear, British Transglobe Expedition/Stone; NASA/Corbis; PA News Photolibrary; Popperfoto; K. Ross/Telegraph Colour Library; Chuck Savage/The Stock Market; F. Siteman/Stone; The Stapleton Collection/Bridgeman Art Library; Vyto Starinskas/Sygma; B. Thomas/Stone; J Tisne/Stone; P. Tweedie/Stone; VCL/N. Clements/Telegraph Colour Library; Jennie Woodcock/Bubbles Photolibrary; Jeff Zaruba/The Stockmarket

CONTENTS

UNIT 1

Tenses
1 Recognizing tenses 1
2 Choosing the correct form 2
3 Correcting mistakes 2

Question forms
4 Making questions with auxiliaries 2
5 Making questions with
   do/does/did 2
6 Question words 3
7 Word order 3
8 Which question word? 3
9 *What* + noun, *How* + adjective
   or adverb 4
10 Replying with a question 4

Vocabulary
11 Jobs 4

Writing
12 Writing an informal letter 5

UNIT 2

Present Simple
1 Making negatives 6
2 Making questions 6
3 Short answers 7
4 Third person singular 7
5 Adverbs of frequency 7

Present Simple or Continuous?
6 Spelling of the present participle 8
7 Choosing the correct form 8
8 *What does she do?* or *What is
   she doing?* 8

have/don't have
9 Making statements and negatives 9
10 Short answers 9

Vocabulary
11 Things in the house 10

Writing
12 Linking words—*but, however,
   so, because,* and 10
13 Describing a person 11

UNIT 3

Past Simple
1 Choosing the right verb 12
2 Making negatives 13

3 Making questions 13
4 Short answers 13
5 Past Simple forms 13
6 Past time expressions 14

Past Continuous
7 Forming the Past Continuous 14
8 Newspaper stories 15

Past Simple or Continuous?
9 Choosing the correct form 15

Vocabulary
10 *have* + noun = activity 16

Writing
11 Linking words—*while, during,*
   and *for* 16
12 Writing a story 1 17

UNIT 4

Count and noncount nouns
1 *a* or *some?* 18
2 *chocolate* or *a chocolate?* 18

Expressions of quantity
3 *some* or *any?* 19
4 *How much...?* or *How many...?* 19
5 *much, many,* or *a lot of?* 19
6 *a few* or *a little?* 20

Articles
7 *a, an,* or *the?* 20
8 No articles 20
9 *a, the,* or nothing? 21

Vocabulary
10 Spelling of plural nouns 21
11 Clothes 21

Writing
12 Filling out forms 22

UNIT 5

Verb patterns
1 Hopes and ambitions 23
2 Infinitive or *-ing*? 24
3 Asking questions 24

***would like (to do)* or *like (doing)*?**
4 *Would you...?* or *Do you...?* 24
5 Choosing the correct form 25
6 *would like* or *like?* 25

will* and *going to
7 Offers and decisions 25
8 What's going to happen? 26
9 Choosing the correct form 26

Vocabulary
10 Words that go together 27

Writing
11 Writing a postcard 28

UNIT 6

What...like?
1 *What is/are...like?* 29
2 *What was/were...like?* 29

Comparatives and superlatives
3 Forming comparatives
   and superlatives 30
4 How old am I? 30
5 Opposite adjectives 31
6 *as* or *than?* 31
7 *as...as/not as...as* 31
8 Making sentences about you 31

Vocabulary
9 Adjective formation 32

Writing—Relative clauses
10 *who/that/which/where* 33
11 Describing a place 33

UNIT 7

Present Perfect
1 Using the Present Perfect 34
2 Making affirmative and negative
   sentences 34
3 Making questions 35
4 Short answers 35
5 Past participles 35
6 *for* or *since?* 36

Tense review
7 Using the correct tense 36
8 Asking questions 36

Vocabulary
9 Men and women 37

Writing—Relative clauses
10 Relative clauses 37
11 Writing a biography 38

This page has been left blank.

1

Tenses • Question forms
Jobs
Writing—an informal letter

Getting to know you

Tenses

1 Recognizing tenses

T 1.1 Complete the texts using the verbs from the box.

can make	's studying
lives	teaches
wants	loves
doesn't have	

1 Enrique (1) __*lives*__ in Puebla, a town in Mexico. He's a student. He (2) _____ medicine because he (3) _____ to be a doctor.
He's married, but he (4) _____ any children. His wife, Silvia, (5) _____ in an elementary school. Enrique (6) _____ cooking.
He (7) _____ excellent tacos!

has	're listening
like	'm sitting
come	'm going to study
live	doesn't work

2 Hi! My name's Rumi and I (1) _____ from Osaka in Japan. I (2) _____ with my parents. My father (3) _____ a job, but my mother (4) _____ . Next year I (5) _____ economics at a university.
I (6) _____ going out with my friends. In the picture I (7) _____ in a club with Noriko and Toshi. We (8) _____ to music.

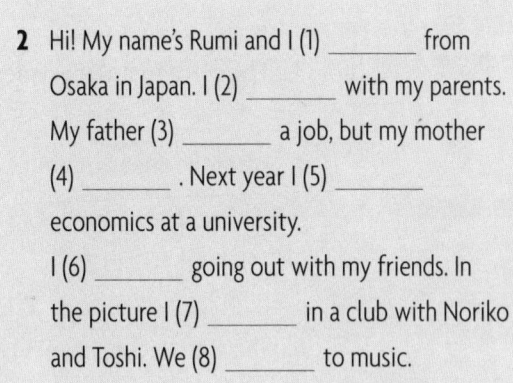

're playing	emigrated
didn't like	have
're going	went
live	was born

3 Bruce is Australian. He (1) _____ in Canada, but he (2) _____ to Australia when he was six. He (3) _____ back to Canada once, but he (4) _____ it because it was so cold after Australia!
He and his brother (5) _____ with their parents in Melbourne. They (6) _____ a big house not far from the beach. 
In the picture he's on the beach with his friends. They (7) _____ volleyball. Tonight he's going out with his girlfriend. They (8) _____ to the movies.

Unit 1 • Getting to know you   1

2 Choosing the correct form

Choose the correct form of the verb.
1. *I'm speaking / (I speak) / I'm speak* three languages: French, Spanish, and English.
2. **A** Where *does Jun come / Jun come / is Jun coming* from?
   B She's Korean. She comes from Seoul.
3. **A** What *you do / do you do / are you doing* tonight?
   B I'm going out.
4. **A** Where's George?
   B He *has / 's taking / take* a shower.
5. **A** What *means this word / does mean this word / does this word mean*?
   B I don't know. Look it up.
6. **A** Do you want a cigarette?
   B No, thanks. I *don't smoke / no smoke / smoke not*.
7. Last year I *went / go / was go* to Canada on vacation.
8. How long *you stay / did you stay / stayed you* in Canada?
9. The weekend was boring. I *no do / didn't / didn't do* anything.
10. **A** I'm going to college next year.
    B What *are you going to / you going to / do you* study?

3 Correcting mistakes

Correct the mistakes in these sentences.
1. ~~At the~~ *On* weekends I'm usually go swimming.
2. Are you enjoy the party?
3. We can't play tennis because it rains.
4. Do you can play chess?
5. How many sisters you have?
6. I no understand what you're saying.
7. What you do tonight?
8. What time you get home last night?
9. Last weekend I see some friends and we have a dinner together.
10. I'm loving American food. It's wonderful!

Question forms

4 Making questions with auxiliaries

T 1.2 Write Yes/No questions for these sentences.
1. She's Brazilian. *Is she Brazilian?*
2. It's raining. _____
3. They're at school. _____
4. They're learning English. _____
5. You're tired. _____
6. She was at home last night. _____
7. I'm right. _____
8. He was born in 1960. _____
9. You can speak Chinese. _____

5 Making questions with *do/does/did*

T 1.3 Write Yes/No questions for these sentences.
1. You like music.
   Do you like music?
2. She comes from Mexico.
   _____
3. They live in an apartment.
   _____
4. You take sugar in your coffee.
   _____
5. I speak English well.
   _____
6. She watched a movie last night.
   _____
7. It started at 8:00.
   _____
8. You want to go home.
   _____
9. He works hard.
   _____

2 Unit 1 · Getting to know you

6 Question words

Match the questions and answers.

1. What do you do?	a. Thirty dollars.
2. Who did you go out with last night?	b. Twenty-five.
	c. Fine. And you?
3. Where do you live?	d. Maria and Pedro.
4. When's your birthday?	e. I'm a teacher.
5. Why are you wearing a suit?	f. *The Daily Times.*
	g. It's today!
6. How many students are there in the class?	h. I'm sure it's mine.
	i. In an apartment in the center of town.
7. How much did you pay for your shoes?	j. Because I'm going to an expensive restaurant.
8. How are you?	
9. Whose money is this?	
10. Which newspaper do you read?	

7 Word order

Put the words in the correct order to make questions. Then answer the questions about you.

1. buy/you/the/did/at/what/store/?

   What did you buy at the store?
   _____

2. is/who/teacher/your/English/?
   _____
   _____

3. parents/now/where/your/right/are/?
   _____
   _____

4. movies/you/go/last/when/did/the/to/?
   _____
   _____

5. learning/you/why/English/are/?
   _____
   _____

6. you/how/to/come/school/do/?
   _____
   _____

7. brothers and sisters/you/many/have/how/do/?
   _____
   _____

8 Which question word?

T 1.4 Complete the conversation with question words.

Kate Hi, Dad.
Dad Morning, Kate. (1) _____ are you today?
Kate Fine, thanks. A little tired.
Dad I didn't hear you come home last night. (2) _____ time did you get in?
Kate About 11:00.
Dad (3) _____ did you go?
Kate Just to Beth's house.
Dad There's a letter for you on the table.
Kate Oh! (4) _____ is it from?
Dad I don't know. Open it and see.
Kate Oh!
Dad (5) _____'s the matter?
Kate Nothing. It's from Luis in Mexico.
Dad That's interesting.
Kate He says he's coming to the United States soon.
Dad (6) _____ ?
Kate Because he's going to study English.
Dad (7) _____ is he going to stay?
Kate Here in San Francisco.
Dad (8) _____ school is he going to?
Kate He doesn't know yet.
Dad (9) _____ is he coming?
Kate Next week.
Dad You should invite him to the house. (10) _____ don't you write back and invite him to dinner on Sunday?
Kate OK, I will. Thanks, Dad.

9 What + noun, How + adjective or adverb

Match a question word in **A** with a word in **B** and a line in **C**. Then answer the questions about you.

A	B	C
How What	color far tall kind much often size long newspaper time	shoes do you take? did you get up this morning? do you read? is it from your house to the center of town? are you? is your hair? do you go swimming? does a hamburger cost in your town? of music do you like? does your English class last?

1. *What color is your hair?*
2. _____
3. _____
4. _____
5. _____
6. _____
7. _____
8. _____
9. _____
10. _____

10 Replying with a question

T 1.5 Write the questions.

1. We had a wonderful vacation.
   Where did you go?

2. I'm reading a good book right now.

3. I bought a new car last week.

4. Nick and I had a great time on Saturday.

5. Ann's going to Taiwan next week.

6. David earns more than $150,000 a year!

7. They have so many children!

Vocabulary

11 Jobs

Add a suffix from the box to the words to make jobs. Change the spelling when necessary. When does the pronunciation change?

| -er/-r | -ian | -ist |

1. music *musician* 2. art _____

3. science _____ 4. journal _____

5. politics _____ 6. manage _____

7. interpret _____ 8. electric _____

9. photograph _____ 10. bake _____

11. library _____ 12. reception _____

Writing

12 Writing an informal letter

1 Look at the organization of this informal letter.

Begin all letters with *Dear ...*, your address, and the date, but not your name.

- Introduction
- Where you live
- Who you live with
- What your family does
- What you do
- What you like
- Your hobbies and interests
- What you're doing these days
- Ending
- You can end a letter to a friend with *Best wishes* or *Regards*, or *Love*, if you know him or her well.
- Your signature

```
                                    38 Clifton Street
                                    Brooklyn, NY

                                    September 27

Dear Maria,

I'm very pleased that we're going to be pen pals.
I'll tell you a little about myself, and you can
do the same when you write to me.
I live in an area of Brooklyn called Brooklyn
Heights. It's near Manhattan, but there are parks
nearby where I take my dog, Mickey, for a walk. I
live with my parents and my younger brother, Paul.
My father works for the post office and my mother
has a part-time job as a nurse.
I go to the local high school, where I have a lot of
friends. I like most subjects, but not all of them!
In the evenings I sometimes visit friends or stay at
home and listen to music, and on weekends I like
going swimming or horseback riding.
These days I'm working very hard because I have
a lot of exams soon, so I'm spending a lot of time
in the library!
I'm looking forward to hearing from you!
Write soon!

Best wishes,

Francis Jones
```

2 Write a similar letter to a pen pal in the United States.

Your pen pal can be male or female.
Write about:
- you
- where you live
- what you do
- your hobbies
- your family

2

Present tenses • *have/don't have*
Things in the house
Writing—describing a person

The way we live

Present Simple

1 **Making negatives**

   T 2.1 Correct the sentences.

   1. The sun rises in the west.
      The sun doesn't rise in the west. It rises in the east.
   2. The president of the United States lives in Alaska.
      _____
   3. Soccer players wear long pants.
      _____
   4. Kangaroos come from Canada.
      _____
   5. The sun shines at night.
      _____
   6. In London people drive on the right.
      _____

2 **Making questions**

   T 2.2 Write the questions.

   1. I get up at _____ .
      What time do you get up?
   2. On weekends I usually go to _____ .
      _____ ?
   3. The bank opens at _____ .
      _____ ?
   4. My mother comes from _____ .
      _____ ?
   5. My children go to _____ school.
      Which _____ ?
   6. My brother works in _____ .
      Where _____ ?
   7. My sister drives a _____ .
      What kind of _____ ?

6 Unit 2 • The way we live

3 Short answers

Answer the questions about you.
Use short answers.

1. Do you play tennis?

   Yes, I do. / No, I don't.

2. Do you like science fiction?

   _____

3. Do you dream a lot?

   _____

4. Do you listen to the radio?

   _____

5. Do your parents read a lot?

   _____

6. Does your teacher give you a lot of homework?

   _____

7. Does it rain a lot in your country?

   _____

4 Third person singular

Write the third person singular of these verbs.

1. help — *helps*
2. watch — *watches*
3. want — _____
4. go — _____
5. carry — _____
6. catch — _____
7. think — _____
8. crash — _____
9. wash — _____
10. read — _____
11. do — _____
12. fly — _____
13. study — _____
14. kiss — _____
15. eat — _____
16. have — _____
17. cry — _____

5 Adverbs of frequency

Put the words in the correct order.

1. movies/you/to/often/go/the/do/how?

   How often do you go to the movies?

2. meat/never/eat/I/because/don't/I/it/like

   _____

3. listen/evening/the/to/parents/radio/the/my/always/in

   _____

4. vacation/how/do/take/often/a/you/?

   _____

5. sometimes/restaurant/we/Japanese/go/a/to

   _____

6. for/late/never/am/school/I

   _____

Present Simple or Continuous?

6 Spelling of the present participle
Write the *-ing* form of these verbs.
1. read — *reading*
2. swim — *swimming*
3. come — *coming*
4. rain — _____
5. wear — _____
6. think — _____
7. shine — _____
8. smoke — _____
9. have — _____
10. take — _____
11. wait — _____
12. get — _____
13. stop — _____
14. run — _____
15. begin — _____

7 Choosing the correct form
Choose the correct form of the verb.
1. I *go /(am going)* to work now. Good-bye!
2. I *read / am reading* a book about astrology.
3. I *read / am reading* lots of books every year.
4. We *go / are going* to a party on Saturday.
5. Nurses *look / are looking* after people in the hospital.
6. Mei-Li *comes / is coming* from Taiwan.
7. She *comes / is coming* for dinner tonight.
8. I *speak / am speaking* four languages.
9. *Do you want / Are you wanting* to go out tonight?

8 *What does she do?* or *What is she doing?*
T 2.3 Look at the picture and answer the questions.

1. What does Wendy do? *She's a nurse.*
2. Is she working in the hospital now? *No, she isn't.*
3. What's she doing? *She's having dinner.*
4. What does Frank do? _____
5. Is he working in a restaurant now? _____
6. What's he doing? _____
7. What does Tony do? _____
8. Is he driving a taxi now? _____
9. What's he doing? _____
10. What does Lisa do? _____
11. Is she working in the kitchen now? _____
12. What's she doing? _____

have/don't have

9 Making statements and negatives

Look at the picture of Jenny's bedroom. Complete the sentences with *has/doesn't have*.

1. She __has__ a CD player.
2. She _____ a tennis racket.
3. She _____ a lot of CDs.
4. She _____ a television.
5. She _____ a computer.
6. She _____ a Walkman.
7. She _____ a cell phone.
8. She _____ many magazines.
9. She _____ a lot of posters.
10. She _____ a sofa.

10 Short answers

T 2.4 Answer the questions about Jenny and about you. Use short answers.

1. Does Jenny have a messy bedroom?
   Yes, she does.
2. Does she have a camera?
   No, she doesn't.
3. Does she have a lot of clothes?
   _____
4. Does she have posters on her walls?
   _____
5. Does she have a computer?
   _____
6. Does she have a lamp in her room?
   _____
7. Do you have a bike?
   _____
8. Do you have a lot of money?
   _____
9. Do you have a CD player?
   _____
10. Do you have a good English accent?
    _____

Write some sentences about your bedroom.

I have a bed, but I don't have a sofa.
I have a radio, but I don't have a TV.
_____
_____
_____
_____

Vocabulary

11 Things in the house

Match the words and pictures.

armchair	sofa	coffee table
bookshelf	carpet	rug
window	curtains	closet
dresser	lamp	mirror

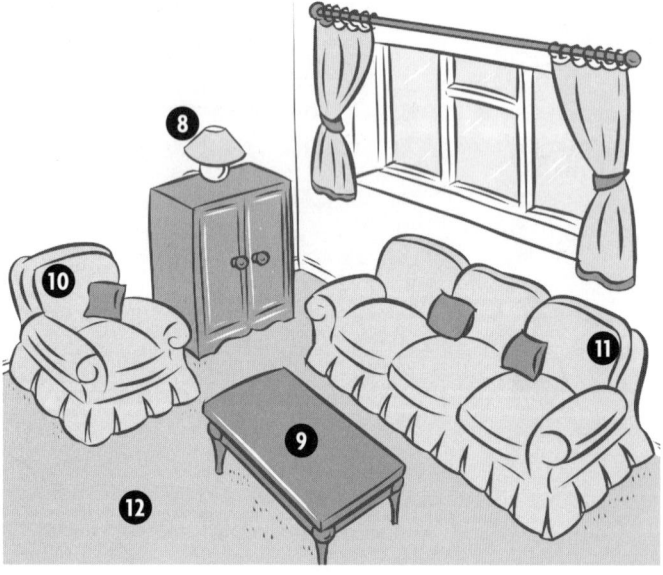

1. _____
2. _____
3. _____
4. _____
5. _____
6. _____
7. _____
8. _____
9. _____
10. _____
11. _____
12. _____

Writing

12 Linking words—*but, however, so, because, and*

1 Complete the sentences with *and*, *so*, or *but*.

1. She can speak French, _____ she can't write it.
2. He's going to work in Colombia, _____ he's learning Spanish.
3. I went into town. I bought some food _____ I went to the library.
4. I don't have a car, _____ I have a motorcycle.
5. She's working late next Friday, _____ she can't come to the party.

> *But* and *however* can contrast ideas, but they are used differently. Compare these sentences. What differences can you see?
> I learned French easily, **but** I didn't like my teacher.
> I learned French easily. **However**, I didn't like my teacher.

2 Join the pairs of sentences in two different ways using *but* and *however*.

1. We enjoyed the vacation. It rained a lot.
   _____
   _____

2. He's moving to Toronto next month. He doesn't like big cities.
   _____
   _____

3. She isn't English. She speaks English perfectly.
   _____
   _____

> *So* is used to express the result of the statement before. *Because* expresses the reason or cause of something.
> **Cause** ——————→ **Result**
> It started to rain, **so** we stopped playing tennis.
> **Result** ←—————— **Cause**
> We stopped playing tennis **because** it started to rain.

10 Unit 2 · The way we live

3 Join the pairs of sentences in two different ways using *so* and *because*.

1. She went home. She was tired.
   a. _____ b. _____
2. We didn't enjoy our vacation. The weather was bad.
   a. _____ b. _____
3. He worked hard. He passed all his exams.
   a. _____ b. _____

13 Describing a person

Complete the text with a linking word from the box.

| and | but | so | because | however |

Two Sisters

My sister and I are very different, (1) _____ we get along well. She likes staying at home in the evening (2) _____ watching television with her boyfriend, (3) _____ I prefer going out with my friends. We like to go to dance clubs or the movies. Sometimes we just go to a cafe. I have exams soon, (4) _____ I'm not going out very much these days. My sister is six years older than I am, (5) _____ she works in a bank. She's trying to save some money (6) _____ she's going to get married this year. Her fiancé's name is Frederick, (7) _____ we all call him Freddy.

People say I look like my sister (8) _____ we both have brown eyes (9) _____ dark hair. (10) _____ , we are very different in character. She's very quiet, (11) _____ I'm a lot more outgoing.

Write a similar short paragraph about yourself and someone in your family.

_____
_____
_____
_____
_____
_____

3

Past Simple • Past Continuous • Past Simple or Continuous
have + noun = activity
Writing—a story 1

It all went wrong

Past Simple

1 Choosing the right verb

Complete the text with a verb from the box in the Past Simple.

fall	find	break
laugh	spend	leave
lose	need	take
celebrate	save	
can't (past = couldn't)		

LOST, ALONE, AND INJURED ON A MOUNTAIN

Yesterday Gary Smith _celebrated_ his twenty-first birthday, but he's lucky to be alive. In March this year, he was mountain climbing, when he (1) _____ his way and (2) _____ 16 hours in sub-zero temperatures.

"My friends (3) _____ at me for having so much survival equipment, but it (4) _____ my life."

On the first night, the weather was so bad that it tore his new mountain tent to pieces, so he moved into a Youth Hostel. He (5) _____ the hostel at 10:00 the next morning, but that afternoon he was in trouble. "I (6) _____ off a rock and (7) _____ my left leg. I (8) _____ move."

Mountain rescue teams went out to look for Gary, and (9) _____ him at 9:00 the next morning. A helicopter (10) _____ him to a hospital, where he (11) _____ several operations. "Next time I'll go with my friends, not on my own!" he joked.

2 Making negatives

T 3.1 Correct the sentences.

1. Shakespeare wrote stories.
   Shakespeare didn't write stories.
   He wrote plays.

2. Christopher Columbus discovered India.
   _____
   _____

3. Beethoven came from France.
   _____
   _____

4. Leonardo da Vinci lived in Mexico.
   _____
   _____

5. Americans landed on the moon in the nineteenth century.
   _____
   _____

6. Buddha came from Australia.
   _____
   _____

3 Making questions

T 3.2 Write the questions.

1. I went to Asia in 19_____ .
   When did you go to Asia?

2. I went to _____ on my last vacation.
   Where _____?

3. We stayed in _____ .
   Where _____?

4. We stayed there for _____ weeks.
   How long _____?

5. We had _____ weather.
   Did _____ good weather?

6. We traveled around by _____ .
   How _____?

7. We had _____ food.
   Did _____ good food?

4 Short answers

Answer the questions about Gary in Exercise 1 and about you. Use short answers.

1. Did Gary get lost?
   Yes, he did.

2. Did he have a lot of equipment?
   _____

3. Did he go with friends?
   _____

4. Did he hurt his hand?
   _____

5. Did you do your homework last night?
   _____

6. Did you play any sports yesterday?
   _____

7. Did it rain yesterday?
   _____

5 Past Simple forms

Write the Past Simple of these verbs.

1. work — *worked*
2. save — *saved*
3. stop — *stopped*
4. come — *came*
5. arrive — _____
6. plan — _____
7. make — _____
8. help — _____
9. use — _____
10. travel — _____
11. feel — _____
12. wash — _____
13. like — _____
14. rob — _____
15. send — _____
16. walk — _____
17. smile — _____
18. clap — _____
19. know — _____

Unit 3 · It all went wrong   13

6 Past time expressions

Complete the sentences with a word from the box. Careful! Sometimes no word is necessary.

ago	last	in	for
at	when	on	

1. I arrived home __at__ six o'clock last night.
2. I saw Jane __—__ yesterday.
3. I was born in Africa _____ 1970.
4. My parents moved back to Canada _____ I was five.
5. We lived in Montreal _____ three years.
6. I left college three years _____ .
7. I found an apartment on my own _____ last year.
8. I usually go home _____ weekends.
9. I didn't go home _____ weekend because some friends came to stay.
10. They arrived _____ three o'clock _____ the afternoon.
11. _____ Saturday night we went out to a concert.
12. _____ we got home we listened to some music.
13. We got up late _____ Sunday morning.
14. _____ the afternoon we went for a walk.
15. I bought a car a few weeks _____ .
16. I had an accident _____ last night.
17. It happened _____ seven o'clock _____ the evening.
18. I took my car to the mechanic _____ this morning.

Past Continuous

7 Forming the Past Continuous

T 3.3 Yesterday you went to a party. This is what you saw when you arrived. Make sentences using the Past Continuous.

When I arrived at the party . . .

1. Jenny/talk/to Mick
   Jenny was talking to Mick.
2. Annie and Pete/dance
   _____
3. Sarah and Bill/sit/on the sofa
   _____
4. Katie/choose/a CD
   _____
5. Max/drink/champagne
   _____
6. Beth and Dave/eat/potato chips
   _____
7. Justin/show/Lucy a picture
   _____
8. Harry/smoke/a cigar
   _____
9. James/tell/a joke
   _____

8 Newspaper stories

Look at the three newspaper stories. Match the phrases with the correct story. Where exactly do they go?

1. ☐ "I was working in the yard at the time," she explained.
2. ☐ ... because they were wearing masks
3. ☐ "I know I was driving fast," he explained to the court.
4. ☐ ... when he was traveling at 120 miles an hour
5. ☐ ... who was coming home from school at the time
6. ☐ The bottom of the tree was slowly moving.

A Motorist Driving at 120 mph

Jeffrey Page

Motorist Jeffrey Page had to pay a fine of $500 in District Court yesterday for speeding. Police stopped him on the highway. The speed limit on highways is 65 miles an hour. "This was because I was late for work." The judge said that this was no excuse.

B TREE DESTROYS HOUSE

Yesterday afternoon a 35-year-old woman narrowly escaped death when a tree blew over and fell onto her house, completely destroying it. "It was very windy. I heard a strange noise coming from our tree. Suddenly the wind blew a little stronger, and I watched the tree crash onto the roof." The Bowles family is staying with friends while their house is being rebuilt.

C POST OFFICE ROBBERY

Yesterday afternoon two robbers stole $700 from a post office in Cavendish, Maine. Police do not have a good description of the two men, but they know that they escaped in a red Ford Escort. This information came from an 11-year-old boy, Charlie Carrack.

The post office in Cavendish

Past Simple or Continuous?

9 Choosing the correct form

Choose the correct form of the verbs.

1. I *met / was meeting* a friend while I *walked / was walking* to class.
2. I *paid / was paying* for my things when I *heard / was hearing* someone call my name.
3. I *turned / was turning* around and *saw / was seeing* Paula.
4. She *wore / was wearing* a bright red coat.
5. We *decided / were deciding* to have a cup of coffee.
6. While we *had / were having* a drink, a waiter *dropped / was dropping* a pile of plates.
7. We all *were / were getting* surprised.
8. While the waiter *picked / was picking* up the broken plates, he *cut / was cutting* his finger.

Unit 3 · It all went wrong   15

Vocabulary

10 have + noun = activity

Have is often used with a noun to express a form of action.
  Where did you **have** lunch?
  Have a nice weekend!
Notice that, with meals, we do not use *a*.
  I **had** breakfast/lunch.

T 3.4 Complete the sentences with a form of *have* and a noun from the box.

drink	argument	look	swim
lunch	breakfast	word	day
game	time	dinner	

1. Would you like to <u>have a drink</u>?
   Yes, please. I'm very thirsty.
2. Did you watch TV last night?
   No, I _____ and went straight to bed.
3. Did you _____ a good _____ of tennis?
   Yes. I won 6–0, 6–2.
4. Bye, Mom. I'm going to the party now!
   Good-bye, darling. _____ a nice _____!
5. Did you _____ this morning?
   No. I got up too late. I just had a cup of coffee.
6. It's noon. Let's _____ and then go shopping.
7. I have a swimming pool in the yard, so if you want to _____ a _____, just come by.
8. Did you _____ a good _____ at the office, dear?
   No, I didn't. The boss was very angry with me.
9. Peter and I always argue. We don't agree about anything. Yesterday we _____ an _____ about politics.
10. I've got my vacation pictures. Do you want to _____ a _____?
11. John! Could I _____ a _____ with you for a minute? There's something I want to talk to you about.

Writing

11 Linking words—*while*, *during*, and *for*

1 *While* is a conjunction and is followed by a clause (subject + verb). If you say "X happened while Y happened," it means X and Y happened at the same time.
  I met Peter **while** I was studying at the university.

2 *During* is a preposition and it is followed by a noun. It has a similar meaning to *while*.
  I worked on a farm **during** my vacation.
  The noun after *during* expresses an activity that takes time.
  during the movie/lesson/afternoon/ soccer game
  While and *during* answer the question *When?*

3 *For* is a preposition and answers the question *How long?* It is followed by a time expression.
  I lived there **for** three years/six months.
  We're taking a vacation **for** two weeks/ a couple of days.

1 Complete the sentences with *while*, *during*, or *for*.
   1. I fell and hurt myself _____ I was playing tennis. It started to rain _____ the match. We played tennis _____ two hours.
   2. I worked in Italy _____ three years. _____ the summer I stayed on a farm in Tuscany. I learned Italian _____ I was there.
   3. We went on vacation to Florida _____ three weeks. _____ the day it was very hot, but it was cool at night. We went to Disney World _____ we were there.
   4. We had a delicious meal yesterday. We sat at the table _____ three hours. _____ the meal we exchanged news. _____ I was talking to Barbara, I learned that Tony was in the hospital.

16 Unit 3 • It all went wrong

2 Read the story and look at the pictures. Complete the text with *while*, *during*, or *for*.

A Disastrous Sailing Vacation

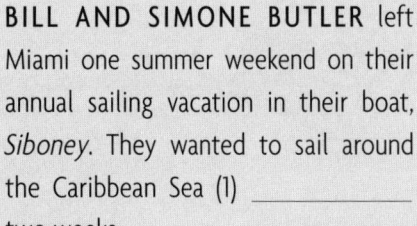

BILL AND SIMONE BUTLER left Miami one summer weekend on their annual sailing vacation in their boat, *Siboney*. They wanted to sail around the Caribbean Sea (1) _____ two weeks.

(2) _____ their vacation, they saw a large group of whales. Bill and Simone were very excited. Unfortunately, (3) _____ they were watching them, the whales began to hit the side of the boat.

Suddenly, water started flooding in, and they realized that they were in trouble. They quickly jumped into the lifeboat (4) _____ the boat was sinking, and watched it disappear under the sea.

Fortunately, they had enough food and water (5) _____ 20 days. They also had a fishing line and a machine which made salt water into drinking water. These two things helped them to survive (6) _____ their terrible experience.

(7) _____ the next 50 days they caught about 10 fish a day and ate them raw. They saw about 20 ships, but although they waved and shouted (8) _____ they were passing by, nobody saw them. They were becoming weaker and weaker. Then, just as they were beginning to lose hope, a fishing boat rescued them. Their disastrous vacation was over.

12 Writing a story 1

Write a story of about 150 words. The story is about a time in your life when everything went wrong. You can choose one of these subjects if you like.

- the day you woke up late for an exam
- a terrible day at work
- an argument with your best friend
- your worst birthday ever
- an awful party

4 Let's go shopping!

Count and noncount nouns • Expressions of quantity
Articles • Plural nouns • Clothes
Writing—filling out forms

1 *a, an,* or *some*?

Put *a,* or *an* before the count nouns, and *some* before the noncount nouns.

1. _a_ chair
2. _some_ sugar
3. ____ stamp
4. ____ book
5. ____ gas
6. ____ tree
7. ____ air
8. ____ money
9. ____ dollar
10. ____ music
11. ____ job
12. ____ work
13. ____ apple
14. ____ fruit
15. ____ tomato
16. ____ tomato soup
17. ____ problem
18. ____ information

Count and noncount nouns

2 *chocolate* or *a chocolate*?

Sometimes a noun can be both a count and noncount noun. Look at the pictures and complete the sentences with *a* + noun or just the noun.

1. I don't like _chocolate_.

2. Would you like _a chocolate_?

3. I need some _____.

4. Can you buy _____?

5. I drink a lot of _____.

6. Let's have _____.

7. Have _____!

8. Have some _____!

9. It's made of _____.

10. Would you like _____ of water?

18 Unit 4 • Let's go shopping!

Expressions of quantity

3 some or any?

Complete the sentences with *some* or *any*.

1. I don't have _____ paper.
2. I'll buy _____ paper when I go to the store.
3. Is there _____ gas in the car?
4. Yes. I put _____ in yesterday.
5. I bought _____ fruit, but they didn't have _____ vegetables.
6. Do you have _____ change? I need 75¢.
7. I saw _____ change on the table a minute ago.
8. I need _____ help with my homework. Are you free?
9. I don't have _____ free time today. Sorry.
10. Did you have _____ problems with this exercise?

4 How much . . . ? or How many . . . ?

T 4.1 Write questions with *How much . . . ?* or *How many . . . ?*

1. We have some eggs.
   How many eggs do we have?
2. We need some flour.
   How much flour do we need?
3. She has a lot of children.
   _____
4. Can you buy some butter?
   _____ want?
5. Their house has a lot of bedrooms.
   _____
6. Some people are coming for dinner on Sunday.
   _____
7. Shakespeare wrote a lot of plays.
   _____
8. She makes a fortune!
   _____

5 much, many, or a lot of?

Look at the picture. Complete the sentences with *much*, *many*, or *a lot of*.

1. There are _a lot of_ apples.
2. The store doesn't have _much_ laundry detergent.
3. There's _____ oil.
4. The store has _____ bottles of water.
5. There isn't _____ frozen food.
6. There isn't _____ candy.
7. The store has _____ cheese.
8. I can see _____ newspapers.
9. But I can't see _____ bread.
10. There isn't _____ yogurt.
11. The store doesn't have _____ birthday cards.
12. But there are _____ grapes!
13. Why aren't there _____ magazines?
14. But there is _____ rice!

Unit 4 • Let's go shopping! 19

6 *a few* or *a little*?

T 4.2 Match a line in **A** with a line in **B** and a line in **C**.

A	B	C
1. Does your tooth hurt?		It takes them about an hour a night.
2. Were there many people at the party?		I'm trying to lose weight.
3. Is there any food left over?		You can borrow them if you want.
4. Do you have any soda?		The children ate most of it.
5. Do you have any books on French literature?	A few.	But I prefer reading.
6. Would you like some cream?		Do you want some ice in it?
7. Are there many Spanish speakers in your class?	A little.	But most of them come from Brazil.
8. Do you watch much TV?		I'll go to the dentist tomorrow.
9. Do you get many letters?		But no one that you know.
10. Do your children get a lot of homework?		But most of them are bills.

Articles

7 *a*, *an*, or *the*?

T 4.3 Complete the sentences with *a*, *an*, or *the*.

1. I bought __a__ hat and __a__ pair of shoes at __the__ mall. Unfortunately _____ shoes are _____ wrong size. I'll take them back tomorrow.
2. **A** Where are _____ children?
   B They're in _____ yard.
3. My sister's _____ teacher in _____ school near Seattle. She has three children, two girls and _____ boy. _____ girls are in her class at school, but _____ boy isn't old enough for school yet.
4. Jane and Bill are _____ very nice couple. She has _____ clothing store, and he works in _____ office in _____ city.
5. **A** Where are my shoes?
   B On _____ floor in _____ kitchen.
6. **A** How much are the driving lessons?
   B Twenty dollars _____ hour.
7. When you come to bed, can you put _____ cat out and turn off _____ lights?
8. I went to _____ restaurant last night.
9. What's _____ name of _____ restaurant we went to last night?

8 No articles

We do not use *a*, *an*, or *the* when we talk about things in general.

Match a noun in **A** with a verb in **B** and a line in **C** to make general statements.

A	B	C
Cows	comes	oil and gas.
Leaves	like	from grapes.
Wood	fall off	grass.
Cats	is	in trees.
Wine	go	full of vitamins.
Birds	live	to school until they're 16.
Children	eat	trees in autumn.
Cars	floats	eating fish.
Fruit	need	on water.

20 Unit 4 • Let's go shopping!

9 *a*, *the*, or nothing?

Complete the sentences with *a*, *the*, or nothing.

1. I come to —— school by —— bus.
2. This morning _____ bus was late.
3. My favorite subject is _____ history, but I'm not very good at _____ math.
4. Ankara is _____ capital of Turkey.
5. I work for _____ company that makes _____ carpets.
6. My friend lives on _____ same street as I do.
7. I was at _____ home all day yesterday.
8. We had _____ a great time in Korea. We're going back there _____ next year.
9. _____ O'Hare is _____ busiest airport in the United States.
10. Leave early if you want to miss _____ rush hour.
11. We arrived in _____ Dallas on _____ third of August.
12. Last night we had _____ dinner in _____ restaurant.
13. I went to _____ bed late.
14. What time does your plane arrive? I'll come to _____ airport to meet you.

Vocabulary

10 Spelling of plural nouns

1 Write the plural form of these nouns.

1. boy _____boys_____
2. lady _____
3. day _____
4. potato _____
5. party _____
6. watch _____
7. glass _____
8. city _____
9. church _____
10. address _____
11. story _____
12. sandwich _____
13. key _____
14. video _____
15. way _____

2 These nouns are irregular. Write the plural forms.

1. child _____
2. person _____
3. woman _____
4. tooth _____
5. sheep _____
6. fish _____

11 Clothes

Write the words.

1. shoes
2.
3.
4.
5.
6.
7.
8.
9.
10.
11.
12.
13.
14.

Unit 4 • Let's go shopping! 21

Writing

12 Filling out forms

1 Match the expressions with the questions.

1. **First name**	a.	Are you married or single?
2. **Last name**	b.	What do you do in your free time?
3. **Date of birth**	c.	What's your phone number?
4. **Place of birth**	d.	What's your first name?
5. **Permanent address**	e.	What do you do?
6. **Marital status**	f.	Where were you born?
7. **Occupation**	g.	When were you born?
8. **Qualifications**	h.	What's your last name?
9. **Hobbies/Interests**	i.	What degrees, diplomas, certificates, etc., do you have?
10. **Telephone number**	j.	Where do you live?

2 Do these things. Write about you.

1. Write your name in capital letters.
   _____

2. Write your signature.
   _____

3. Delete where not applicable.
   (Mr./Mrs./Miss/Ms.)

4. Write your zip code.
   _____

3 Complete the form.

The Oak Tree School of English — *Enrollment form*

PLEASE USE CAPITAL LETTERS

- Mr./Mrs./Ms.* _____
- First name _____
- Nationality _____
- Address in your country _____
  _____
  _____
- Last name _____
- Date of birth _____
- Language(s) _____
- Occupation _____
- Date of arrival _____
- Date of departure _____

Reason for learning English: Business/pleasure/exams/other *(If other, please specify.) _____

How many hours a day do you want to study? _____

How long are you going to stay at the school? _____

What date do you want to start? _____

Signature _____

*Delete where not applicable.

5

Verb patterns • *will* and *going to*
Words that go together
Writing—a vacation postcard

What do you want to do?

Verb patterns

1 Hopes and ambitions

Write a sentence about each of these people's ambitions.

1. Sheila/teacher/work/with children
   Sheila wants to be a teacher because she likes working with children.
   Sheila hopes to be a teacher because she loves working with children.
   Sheila would like to be a teacher because she enjoys working with children.

2. Jane/vet/work/with animals
   _____
   _____

3. Mark/farmer/he/outside in the fresh air
   _____
   _____

4. Suzy/stockbroker/want/make/a lot of money
   _____
   _____

5. Maya/do volunteer work/help/children in developing countries
   _____
   _____

6. Jan/accountant/work/with numbers
   _____
   _____

7. My father/retire next year/want/have more free time
   _____
   _____

8. My parents/buy/a house by the ocean/sail
   _____
   _____

Unit 5 • What do you want to do?   23

2 Infinitive or -ing?

Complete the sentences with the correct form of the verb, the infinitive or -ing. Sometimes both are possible.

1. I enjoy _walking_ (walk) in the rain.
2. Would you like _to have_ (have) something to eat?
3. I want _____ (see) a movie on TV tonight.
4. I hope _____ (make) some money soon.
5. When did you finish _____ (paint) the kitchen?
6. I began _____ (learn) English when I was seven.
7. Some people like _____ (have) breakfast in bed, but I don't.
8. Don't forget _____ (mail) my letter!
9. We've decided _____ (get) married in the spring.
10. When she saw how I was dressed, she started _____ (laugh).
11. What do you want _____ (do) tonight?
12. I'd like _____ (go) to the theater.
13. I love _____ (listen) to live music.
14. She continued _____ (talk) during the whole meal.

3 Asking questions

T 5.1 Write B's questions and complete A's answers.

1. **A** I hope to go to college.
   B What/want/study/?
   What do you want to study?
   A _I want to study_ _____ math.
2. **A** Carol called while you were out.
   B What/want/talk about/?
   _____
   A _____ a problem she's having.
3. **A** I quit my job yesterday.
   B Why/decide/do that/?
   _____
   A _____ because it was boring.
4. **A** I'm going to bed early because I have a plane to catch tomorrow.
   B What time/want/leave the house/?
   _____
   A _____ as early as possible.
5. **A** That book you lent me was great!
   B When/finish/read/it/?
   _____
   A _____ last night.
6. **A** I don't want to go out tonight.
   B What/would like/do/?
   _____
   A _____ stay at home and go to bed early.

would like (to do) or like (doing)?

4 Would you ...? or Do you ...?

T 5.2 Match the questions and answers.

1. Would you like to watch TV?	a. Yes, especially movies and cartoons.
2. Would you like something to eat?	b. Yes, I'd love to. What time?
3. Do you like parties?	c. No. There's nothing good on tonight.
4. Do you like french fries?	d. I'm afraid I don't. I think they're noisy, and there are usually too many people.
5. Do you like watching TV?	e. No. I think they're very bad for you.
6. Would you like to come to a party on Saturday?	f. No, thanks. I'm not hungry.

24 Unit 5 · What do you want to do?

5 Choosing the correct form

Check (✓) the correct form of the verb.

1. **A** ✓ Would you like a drink?
   ☐ Do you like a drink?
   B Yes, please. I'll have an orange juice.
2. **A** ☐ Do you like your teacher?
   ☐ Would you like your teacher?
   B Yes, she's very nice.
3. **A** ☐ Do you like going for walks?
   ☐ Would you like to go for a walk?
   B Yes, I often go for a walk at night.
4. **A** ☐ Do you like swimming?
   ☐ Would you like to go for a swim?
   B What a good idea! It's so hot today!
5. **A** ☐ What do you like doing on weekends?
   ☐ What would you like to do this weekend?
   B I like putting my feet up and relaxing. Sometimes I play tennis.
6. **A** ☐ What do you like to do in the evening?
   ☐ What would you like to do this evening?
   B Why don't we stop by and see Pat and Peter?

6 *would like* or *like*?

T 5.3 Complete the sentences with *would like* (*to do*) or *like* (*doing*) and the correct form of the verb.

1. **A** What kind of books ___do___ you ___like reading___ (read)?
   B I _____ biographies and mysteries.
2. **A** _____ you _____ (be) a teacher when you grow up?
   B No. They don't make very much and they work very hard.
3. **A** It's Sophie's birthday soon.
   B Is it? What _____ she _____ (get) for a present?
   A Well, I know she _____ (cook). Why don't you buy her a new cookbook?
4. My daughter has a lot of pens and pencils. She _____ (draw).
5. My son is a very fast runner. He says that one day he _____ (run) in the Olympic Games.

will and *going to*

7 Offers and decisions

Look at the pictures. What are the people saying? Make sentences with *will*.

❶ _____

❷ _____

❸ _____

❹ _____

8 What's going to happen?

Look at the pictures. What's going to happen? Make sentences with *is/are going to* + verb.

1. *It's going to rain.*
2. _____
3. _____
4. _____
5. _____
6. _____
7. _____

9 Choosing the correct form

T 5.4 Choose the correct form of the verb.

1. **A** Why are you working so hard these days?
   B Because *I'll buy / I'm going to buy* a car, so I'm saving as much as I can.
2. **A** What *will you buy / are you going to buy* Jill for her birthday?
   B A CD.
   A She doesn't have a CD player.
   B Oh. *I'll buy / I'm going to buy* her a book, then.
3. **A** Dad, can you fix this for me?
   B I can't, sorry. Ask Mom. *She'll do / She's going to do* it for you.
4. **A** Why do you have so many eggs?
   B Because *I'll make / I'm going to make* an omelette.
5. **A** What *will you do / are you going to do* today?
   B It's John's birthday, so *I'll make / I'm going to make* him a cake.
6. **A** I have an appointment with the bank manager this morning.
   B Why *will you see / are you going to see* him?
   A Because my husband and I *will start / are going to start* our own business, and we need some money.
7. **A** I don't have enough money to get home.
   B *I'll lend / I'm going to lend* you some, if you like. How much do you want?
   A Five dollars is enough. *I'll pay / I'm going to pay* you back tomorrow.

26 Unit 5 · What do you want to do?

Vocabulary

10 Words that go together

1 Match a verb in **A** with a line in **B**.

A	B
1. wear *f*	a. the dishes
2. tell ___	b. a story
3. drive ___	c. a picture
4. take ___	d. a check
5. do ___	e. a van
6. make ___	f. a suit
7. cash ___	g. a phone call
8. mail ___	h. a suitcase
9. ride ___	i. a taxi
10. pack ___	j. a meal
11. pay ___	k. a letter
12. order ___	l. a movie on TV
13. watch ___	m. a horse
14. take ___	n. a bill

2 Complete the sentences with a preposition from the box.

| for | at | in | to | with | of |

1. I'm waiting *for* the mail carrier to arrive.
2. Look ____ that picture! Isn't it beautiful!
3. I'm looking ____ Mary. Is she here?
4. My brother works ____ IBM.
5. If you have a problem, ask ____ help.
6. Are you interested ____ history?
7. Did you know that Helen is getting married ____ James?
8. Can I speak ____ you for a minute?
9. I agree ____ you about most things, but not politics.
10. My children are afraid ____ dogs.
11. Are you good ____ tennis?
12. This guidebook is full ____ useful information.

Unit 5 · What do you want to do?   27

Writing

11 Writing a postcard

1. Read the postcard. What is the only adjective used by Bill and Sue?

2. Bill and Sue use *nice* eight times. Complete the sentences below with a better adjective from the box. Use each adjective once only.

   Careful! Sometimes more than one word is possible, but not always!

wonderful	small	terrible
comfortable	old	good
spectacular	long	

   1. We're having a _____ time here in Colorado.
   2. But the weather is _____ .
   3. We're staying in a _____ hotel near a _____ town.
   4. We have _____ views of the mountains.
   5. Mesa Verde was really _____ .
   6. We're hoping to go for a _____ walk by the lake.
   7. Did you have a _____ time in Alaska?

Dear Laura,
  We're having a nice time here in Colorado, but the weather isn't very nice. We're staying in a nice hotel near a nice town called Durango. We have nice views of the mountains and forests from our bedroom. Yesterday we went to see Mesa Verde. It was really nice. Today we are hoping to go for a nice walk by the lake. Did you have a nice time in Alaska? We'll call you next week.
  Love,
  Bill and Sue XXXX

Laura Green
612 Lawrence Lane
Wayne, PA 19987

3. Where were you on your last vacation? Imagine you are still there. Write a postcard to a friend in the United States, but use the adjective *nice* only once!

   Write about these things.
   - the weather
   - the accommodations
   - something you did yesterday
   - something you are going to do today

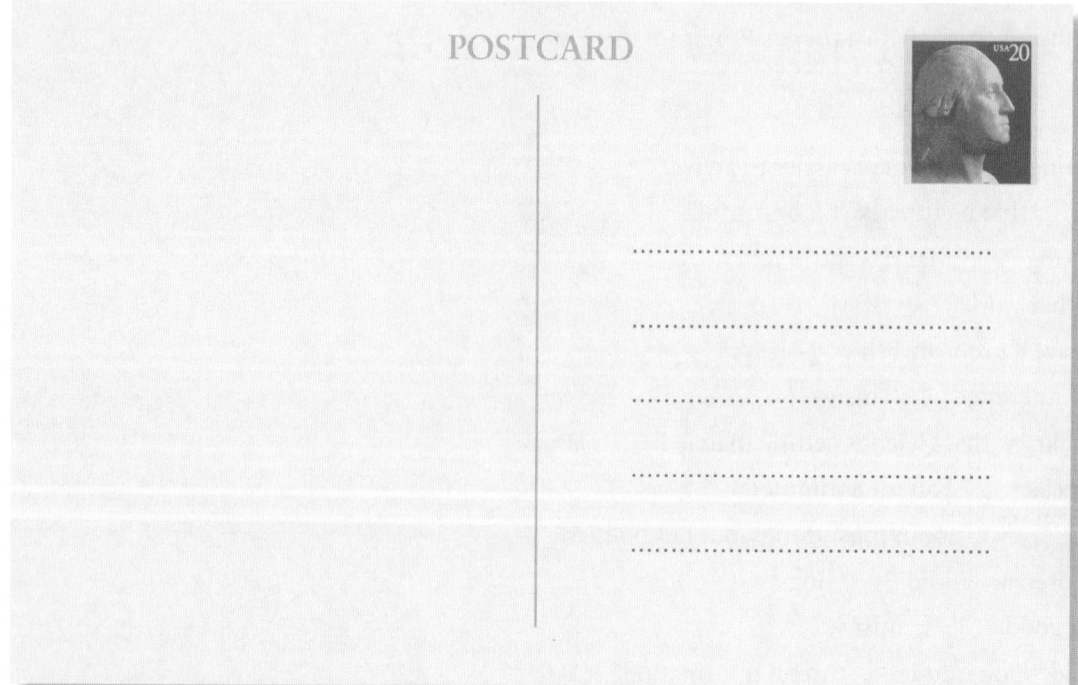

What...like? • Comparatives and superlatives
Adjective formation
Writing—describing a place

The best in the world

What...like?

1 What is/are...like?

1 Your friend is living in Australia for a year. Ask questions about the country.

1. the weather
   What's the weather like?

2. the countryside

3. the people

4. the towns

5. Sydney

6. the beaches

7. the TV programs

2 **T 6.1** Match a question in Exercise 1 with an answer.

   a. ☐ There aren't many. They're mainly on the coast.
   b. [1] It's hot nearly all year round.
   c. ☐ It's a spectacular place. The Opera House is fantastic.
   d. ☐ There are millions of sheep and a lot of desert.
   e. ☐ They have beautiful white sand, and are miles long.
   f. ☐ They're really nice and friendly.
   g. ☐ They're a lot like the ones at home.

2 What was/were...like?

T 6.2 Complete the questions about Robert's terrible vacation.

1. **A** What _____was the hotel_____ like?
   B Awful. My room was tiny, and the service was bad.

2. **A** What _____ like?
   B It was terrible. I waited over six hours for the plane.

3. **A** What _____ like?
   B Miserable! It rained every day!

4. **A** What _____ like?
   B They were crowded and dirty. There was no sand on them, just stones!

5. **A** What _____ like?
   B Disgusting! French fries with everything and they didn't cook them very well.

Unit 6 • The best in the world 29

Comparatives and superlatives

3 Forming comparatives and superlatives

Look at this extract from the *Oxford American Wordpower Dictionary*. It shows when an adjective with a consonant doubles in the comparative and superlative forms.

big /bɪg/ adj. (bigger, biggest)
1 large: *Denver is a big city.*
2 important: *I have some big news!*

Look at your dictionary. Does it give the same information? Write the comparative and superlative forms of these adjectives.

happy	*happier*	*happiest*
beautiful		
new		
neat		
hot		
good		
handsome		
mean		
generous		

thin		
busy		
patient		
young		
bad		
comfortable		
rude		
sad		
large		

4 How old am I?

Read the text and answer the questions.

I have two sisters, Abigail and Jill, and two brothers, Gordon and Robert. Abigail is twenty. Jill is six years younger than Abigail, but she is two years older than Robert. Robert is four years younger than I am, and he is eight years younger than Gordon.

1. How old am I?
   _____.

2. Who is the youngest in the family?
   _____.

3. How old is Robert?
   _____.

4. Is Jill older than I am?
   _____.

5. Am I the oldest in the family?
   _____.

6. Who are the twins?
   _____.

30 Unit 6 · The best in the world

5 Opposite adjectives

T 6.3 Complete the sentences with an opposite adjective in its comparative or superlative form.

1. Robert is the oldest in the family.
   No, he isn't. He's _the youngest_ .
2. Bob is more polite than his brother.
   No, he isn't. He's _____ .
3. I'm the tallest in this class!
   No, you aren't. You're _____ .
4. My homework was worse than yours.
   No, it wasn't. It was _____ .
5. The weather today is colder than yesterday.
   No, it isn't. It's _____ .
6. She bought the cheapest watch in the store.
   No, she didn't. She bought _____ .
7. Jack's meaner than Alan.
   No, he isn't. He's _____ .
8. Janet arrived later than John.
   No, she didn't. She arrived _____ .
9. This is the easiest exercise in this book.
   No, it isn't. It's _____ .

6 as or than?

Complete the sentences with *as* or *than*.

1. Are you as tall __as__ your brother?
2. She's not as smart _____ her sister.
3. Was Joan's party better _____ Maria's?
4. I'm studying the same subject _____ Emma.
5. Liz works much harder _____ John.
6. I don't have as many cousins _____ you.

7 as ... as/not as ... as

T 6.4 Rewrite the sentences with *as ... as* or *not as ... as*.

1. Bob's taller than Jack.
   Jack's not as tall as Bob.
2. Bob got more presents than Jack.
   Jack didn't get as many presents as Bob.
3. Jill's more intelligent than Bill.
   Bill's not _____ .
4. The sun's hotter than the moon.
   The moon isn't _____ .
5. Are you and your husband the same age?
   Are you _____ your husband?
6. You can read more quickly than I can.
   I can't _____ .
7. Harry won more money than Bill.
   Bill didn't win _____ .
8. "Is Brazil bigger than Colombia?" "Yes, it is."
   "Is Colombia _____ ?"
   "No, it isn't."
9. Eva's work is better than mine.
   My work isn't _____ .
10. Dogs are friendlier than cats.
    Cats aren't _____ .

8 Making sentences about you

Write nine sentences about you and your family. (Three comparatives, three superlatives, and three with *as ... as*.)

I'm more hardworking than my sister.
My grandfather is the oldest.
I'm not as patient as my mother.

_____
_____
_____
_____
_____
_____
_____
_____
_____

Unit 6 · The best in the world

Vocabulary

9 Adjective formation

1 Use the suffixes in the box to write the adjectives formed from these nouns. They have all appeared in Unit 6 of the Student Book.

| -y | -ed | -ing | -al | -ful | -ate | -ial | -ous | -ent | -tic |

Noun	Adjective	Noun	Adjective
1. success	successful	10. wealth	_____
2. luck	_____	11. generosity	_____
3. romance	_____	12. mess	_____
4. wind	_____	13. noise	_____
5. difference	_____	14. dirt	_____
6. happiness	_____	15. pollution	_____
7. depression	_____	16. finance	_____
8. health	_____	17. medicine	_____
9. person	_____	18. fortune	_____

2 Complete the sentences with an adjective from Exercise 1.
1. My dad's really _____ . He's always buying presents for everyone.
2. Before you can get a credit card, you have to provide a lot of _____ details.
3. I try to lead a _____ lifestyle—lots of exercise, fruit, and no junk food.
4. The dance club was so _____ that you couldn't hear yourself speak.
5. After the earthquake, the country needed a lot of _____ equipment to look after the sick and wounded.
6. She had a car accident, but she was _____ to escape with no injuries at all.
7. Venice is a very _____ city. A lot of people go their on honeymoon.
8. Here is the _____ news. Share prices on the Dow Jones Index have fallen dramatically.
9. After a heart attack, he needed major surgery, but fortunately the operation was _____ .
10. I didn't like that city at all. The streets were so _____ and the air was so _____ .

32 Unit 6 · The best in the world

Writing—Relative clauses

10 who/that/which/where

> We use *who*, *that*, *which*, and *where* to join sentences.
> *Who*, *that*, *which*, and *where* are relative pronouns. Look at these sentences.
>
> I met the man. **He** works in the bank.
> I met the man **who** works in the bank.
> **who = person/people**
>
> I bought the coat. **It** was in the store window.
> I bought the coat **which/that** was in the store window.
> **which/that = thing/things**
>
> The hotel was very comfortable. We stayed **in it**.
> The hotel **where** we stayed was very comfortable.
> **where (in which) = place**

Join the sentences with the correct relative pronoun.

1. There's the boy. He broke the window.
   There's the boy who broke the window.

2. That's the school. He teaches at it.
   _____

3. There are the police officers. They caught the thief.
   _____

4. He gave her a watch. It stopped after two days.
   _____

5. The Red Lion is a restaurant. We met in it for dinner.
   _____

6. Here are the letters. They arrived this morning.
   _____

7. That's the house. I was born in it.
   _____

8. Where is the woman? She ordered the fish.
   _____

11 Describing a place

1 Read the description of a town. Complete it with *who*, *which*, or *where*.

MY HOMETOWN

I WAS BORN IN BOULDER, a city west of Denver, Colorado. Boulder, (1) _____ is at the foothills of the Rocky Mountains, is a small city with a population of about 90,000 people. The University of Colorado is in Boulder, and the National Center for Atmospheric Research (2) _____ scientists from all over the world work is also there. Boulder attracts students, scientists, and world-class athletes (3) _____ all enjoy Boulder's natural beauty.

It is not unusual to see world-class runners and bicyclists training in and around Boulder. The athletes, (4) _____ come to train in Boulder because it is more than a mile above sea level, often end up making Boulder their home long after their athletic careers are over.

I moved from Boulder ten years ago but often return. I miss the people, (5) _____ are so relaxed and friendly, and I miss the wild, beautiful landscape near the city, (6) _____ there are so many mountain trails and streams. Boulder is a city (7) _____ will always remain in my heart.

2 Write a similar description of your hometown in about 200 words.
First write some facts about it.
- Where is it?
- Is it big or small?
- What buildings and industries does it have?

Next write some personal opinions.
- Do you like it?
- Why?

7

Present Perfect • Tense review
Men and women
Writing—completing a biography

Fame

Present Perfect

1 Using the Present Perfect

T 7.1 Complete the text with a verb from the box in the Present Perfect.

| travel | meet | hunt | have |
| ride | see | live | be (x4) | do |

My grandfather is 96 years old, and he (1) *has had* a long and interesting life. He (2) _____ a lot, especially in Asia. He (3) _____ the Taj Mahal in India, and the Pyramids in Egypt. He (4) _____ lions in Africa, and (5) _____ a camel across the Sahara Desert. He says that the most beautiful place he (6) _____ to is Kathmandu in Nepal. He (7) _____ many famous people in his lifetime, including tha Dalai Lama and Mahatma Gandhi.

He (8) _____ married twice. His first wife died when she was 32. He met his second wife while he was traveling around France by bike. He and his wife, Eleanor, (9) _____ married for 50 years, and they (10) _____ in the same house in the country since they got married. He says that he (11) _____ never _____ sick in his life. The secret of good health, according to my grandfather, is exercise. He goes swimming every day. He (12) _____ this since he was a boy. He also has a glass of whiskey every night! Perhaps that is his secret!

2 Making affirmative and negative sentences

Make sentences about these people.
1. Alice is a journalist.
   meet/a lot of famous people
   She has met a lot of famous people.
   not be/on television
   She hasn't been on television.
2. Robert Swan is an explorer.
   be /North Pole
   _____
   see/polar bears
   _____
   never/get lost
   _____

34 Unit 7 • Fame

3. Bill and Sonia are unemployed.

   not have/a job for six months

   _____

   not take/a vacation since Christmas

   _____

   not be/the movies for a year

   _____

4. Sandra is a tennis player.

   play/since she was six

   _____

   not win/a senior competition

   _____

   never play/at Wimbledon

   _____

3 Making questions

1 Ask these people questions about their experiences.

1. **a race-car driver**—have an accident?

   Have you ever had an accident?

2. **an explorer**—get lost?

3. **an actress**—forget your lines?

4. **a mountaineer**—climb Mount Everest?

5. **a window cleaner**—fall off your ladder?

6. **a pop singer**—have a number-one song?

7. **an electrician**—have an electric shock?

2 **T 7.2** Now match these answers to the questions in Exercise 1.

a. ☐ Yes, I have, once! I was so embarrassed!
b. ☐ No, I haven't yet, but I reached number 10 with my last one.
c. ☐ No, I haven't. I've always had a good team to help me.
d. ☐ Yes, I have, lots of times! But not a serious crash.
e. ☐ Yes, I have, unfortunately. I broke my leg.
f. ☐ No, I haven't, fortunately. I'm very careful about safety.
g. ☐ No, I haven't yet, but I would like to.

4 Short answers

T 7.3 Answer the questions about "My grandfather" in Exercise 1 and about you. Use short answers.

1. Has your grandfather been married for a long time?
   Yes, he has.

2. Has he ever met a famous person?

3. Has he often been sick?

4. Have he and his wife lived in their house for a long time?

5. Has he had an interesting life?

6. Have you ever been to Mexico?

7. Have you ever tried Chinese food?

8. Has your teacher ever been angry with you?

9. Have you ever forgotten to do your homework?

5 Past participles

Write the past participle of these verbs.

1. walk   *walked*
2. come   _____
3. write   _____
4. win   _____
5. sell   _____
6. try   _____
7. read   _____
8. play   _____
9. find   _____
10. visit _____
11. stop   _____
12. study _____
13. die   _____
14. do   _____

6 *for* or *since*?

Complete the sentences with *for* or *since*.

1. I haven't seen Keith *for* a while.
2. He's been in China _____ January.
3. He works for a company called KMP. He has worked for them _____ several years.
4. He and his wife have lived next to me _____ their son, Tom, was born.
5. I have known them _____ many years.
6. We have been friends _____ we were at college together.
7. His wife, Carrie, is a designer. She has had her own studio _____ six months.
8. I'm taking care of Tom today. He's been at my house _____ 8:00 this morning.

Tense review

7 Using the correct tense

Put the verb in parentheses in the correct tense, Present Perfect, Past Simple, or Present Simple.

John Grisham

John Grisham (1) _____ (be) an author. His first career (2) _____ (help) him become an author. He (3) _____ (graduate) from law school at Mississippi State University in 1981 and (4) _____ (begin) to work as a lawyer. One day he overheard a criminal case and decided to start a novel about what might have happened. He (5) _____ (finish) his first novel, *A Time to Kill*, in 1988 after he (6) _____ (spend) three years writing it.

Since publishing *A Time to Kill* in 1988, Grisham (7) _____ (write) one novel a year. All of his novels (8) _____ (become) best-sellers. There (9) _____ (be) currently over 60 million John Grisham books in print worldwide, which have been translated into 29 languages.

Grisham is married to Renée, his wife of 16 years. They have two children. The family (10) _____ (divide) their time between a farm in Mississippi and a plantation near Charlottesville, Virginia.

8 Asking questions

T 7.4 Write the questions about John Grisham.

1. What *does he do* ? He's an author.
2. What _____? His first career.
3. When _____? In 1981.
4. What _____? A lawyer.
5. When _____? In 1988.
6. How long _____? Three years.
7. How many _____? One a year.
8. How many _____? All of his novels.
9. How many _____? Sixty million.
10. What _____? Renée.
11. Where _____? In Mississippi and Virginia.

Vocabulary

9 Men and women

1 Many nouns refer to both men and women.
  student doctor teacher

  Some words refer to one sex only.
  actress waiter king

  Put the words in the correct column.

nephew	musician	teenager
chef	bridegroom	professor
actor	uncle	pilot
niece	model	cousin
aunt	athlete	bride
child	sir	flight attendant
madam	nurse	

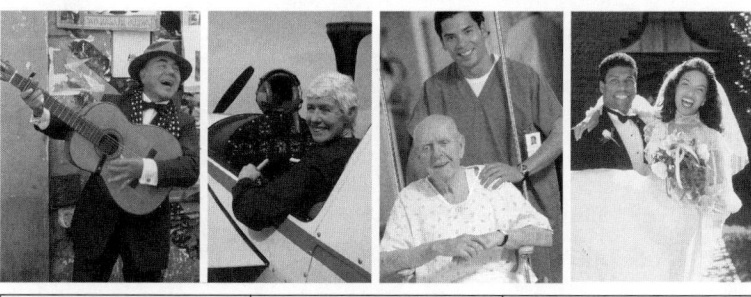

Men	Women	Both
nephew		

2 Complete the sentences with a word from Exercise 1.

  1. He's my sister's son. He's my _nephew_ .
  2. I run in races. I'm an _____ .
  3. In my job I wear the latest fashions. I'm a _____ .
  4. I serve you drinks on a plane flight. I'm a _____ .
  5. I teach at a university. I'm a _____ .
  6. I cook food for a restaurant. I'm a _____ .
  7. The wedding was wonderful. The _____ looked beautiful, and the _____ was very handsome.
  8. "Good evening, _____ . Good evening, _____ . Here is the menu."

Writing

10 Relative clauses

who/which/that as the object

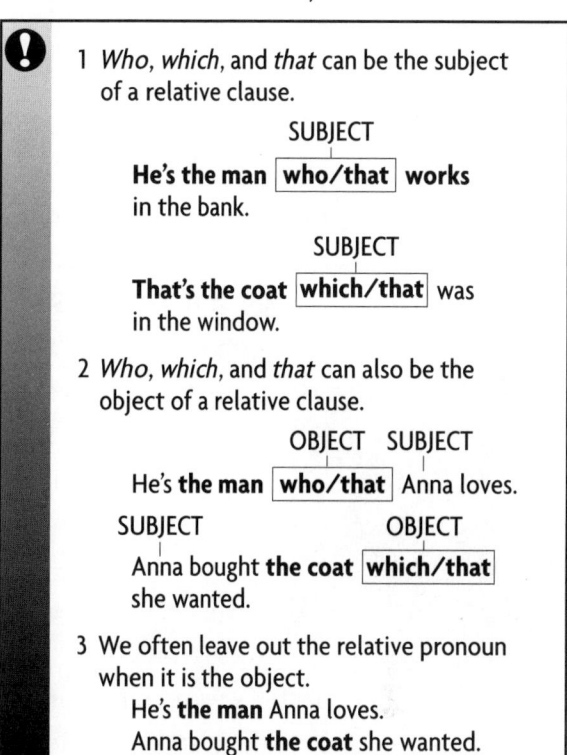

> 1 *Who*, *which*, and *that* can be the subject of a relative clause.
>
>   He's the man [who/that] works in the bank. (SUBJECT)
>
>   That's the coat [which/that] was in the window. (SUBJECT)
>
> 2 *Who*, *which*, and *that* can also be the object of a relative clause.
>
>   He's the man [who/that] (OBJECT) Anna loves (SUBJECT).
>
>   Anna bought (SUBJECT) the coat [which/that] (OBJECT) she wanted.
>
> 3 We often leave out the relative pronoun when it is the object.
>
>   He's **the man** Anna loves.
>   Anna bought **the coat** she wanted.

Complete the sentences with *who*, *which*, or *that*. If it is possible to leave the relative pronoun out, put parentheses around it.

1. He's the man _(who/that)_ Anna loves.
2. The actor gave a party _____ cost $20,000.
3. The man _____ you met at the party was a famous actor.
4. What's the name of the woman _____ was wearing the gold dress?
5. You're reading the book _____ I wanted to read.
6. There's someone at the door _____ wants to speak to George.
7. I don't like food _____ is very spicy.
8. That's the dictionary _____ Bill gave me for my birthday.
9. Those are old cars _____ only take leaded gas.
10. Do you like the people _____ Sarah invited to her party?

11 Writing a biography

1 Complete the biography of Cher with *who*, *which*, or *where*.

Cher

Cher was born in the United States on May 20, 1946, in El Centro, (1) *which* is on the California/Mexico border. Her full name is Cherilyn Sarkisian and she is part Cherokee, and part Armenian, Turkish, and French. She left high school when she was 16 and went to Los Angeles, (2) _____ she planned to take acting lessons. There she met Salvatore Bono, (3) _____ was working at the Gold Star Studios (4) _____ Phil Spector was recording many famous singers. He discovered that Cher could sing, and they became the singing duo Sonny and Cher. Their first hit song was "I Got You, Babe," (5) _____ topped the charts in 1965. Cher was still only 19. They got married and had a daughter, (6) _____ they named Chastity. In 1975 Sonny and Cher were divorced, and later that year Cher married Greg Allmann, (7) _____ was another famous rock star. They had a son named Elijah Blue. But two years later Cher was divorced for the second time because of Allman's drug and alcohol problems. She decided to turn to acting again. In 1982 she appeared in her first major movie, *Come Back to the Five and Dime, Jimmy Dean, Jimmy Dean*, (8) _____ was well received by the critics and public. She went on to win Best Actress at the Cannes Film Festival in 1985 for her role in *Mask*, and finally she won an Oscar for *Moonstruck* in 1987. However, in the 1990s she returned to pop music in a big way. She has had three number-one hits from her chart-topping album "Believe," (9) _____ has reached a whole new audience. In her long career, Cher has been extremely successful both as a serious actress and as a pop star, (10) _____ is an extraordinary achievement.

2 Divide the text into five paragraphs according to these headings:
- introduction
- early career
- private life
- later career
- life now

3 Write a similar biography of somebody who you think is interesting.

Review

Tenses and verb forms

Question forms

1 Word order

Put the words in the right order to ask a question, and write true answers.

1. from you where are
   Where are you from ?   _I'm from Detroit._

2. it now raining right is
   _____ ?
   _____

3. Chinese ever you food eaten have
   _____
   _____ ?

4. are going do you this to what weekend
   _____ ?
   _____

5. time up get usually do what you
   _____
   _____ ?

6. many you can how languages speak
   _____ ?
   _____

7. start English when you studying did
   _____
   _____ ?

2 Short answers

Complete the questions in **A**. Then match a question in **A** and an answer in **B**.

A	B
Does he come from Brazil?	Yes, you are.
_____ he coming this evening?	No, she hasn't.
_____ I late?	Yes, he is.
_____ she have a car?	No, we aren't.
_____ we going by car?	Yes, we did.
_____ she work in a bank?	No, you don't.
_____ I need a passport?	No, she doesn't.
_____ we see him yesterday?	Yes, he does.

3 Correcting mistakes

In each of the following questions there is one mistake. Find it and correct it.

1. What you do?   _What do you do_ ?
2. Does he got a calculator?
   _____ ?
3. Have you ever ride a motorcycle?
   _____ ?
4. What you are doing tonight?
   _____ ?
5. Where you went last night?
   _____ ?
6. Your friends they like traveling?
   _____ ?
7. Do you can speak English?
   _____ ?
8. What are you go to do tomorrow?
   _____ ?

Present Simple

1 Making questions

Write questions and answers.

1. he/get up—6:00
   What time does he get up ?
   He gets up at 6:00.

2. she/do—architect
   _____ ?
   _____

3. they/live—Toronto
   _____ ?
   _____

4. Mark/study—physics
   _____ ?
   _____

5. bank / open—9:00

   _____ ?

6. her parents / come from—Minnesota

   _____ ?

7. she / speak—Russian and Chinese

   _____ ?

2 Making negatives

Make the following sentences negative. Then give the right information.

1. Lions live in Europe.
   Lions don't live in Europe. They live in Africa.

2. Tiger Woods play tennis.

3. Birds build nests underground.

4. Tea comes from Canada.

5. The temperature rises at night.

6. Zoologists study rocks.

7. Brazilians speak Spanish.

3 Present Simple or Continuous?

Underline the correct verb form in the following sentences.

1. He *speaks* / *'s speaking* French and German.
2. I *don't understand* / *'m not understanding*.
3. Hurry up! I *wait* / *'m waiting*.
4. What sports *do you like* / *are you liking*?
5. We *come* / *'re coming* to see you this weekend.
6. "What *do you do* / *are you doing*?"
   "I *write* / *'m writing* a postcard."
7. *Do Americans drive* / *Are Americans driving* on the left?
8. "*Do you enjoy* / *Are you enjoying* the movie?"
   "Yes, I *do* / *am*."
9. "*Does she need* / *Is she needing* any help?"
   "No, she *doesn't* / *isn't*."

Past Simple

1 Describing a vacation

Put the verb in parentheses in the Past Simple.

David Where *did you go* (go) for your last vacation, Sara?
Sara I (1) _____ (go) cycling in Arizona with two friends.
David Oh, yes? How (2) _____ (get) to Arizona?
Sara We (3) _____ (take) a train from San Diego.
David (4) _____ (stay) in hotels?
Sara Only twice, when the weather (5) _____ (not be) very good. The rest of the time we (6) _____ (camp), so we (7) _____ (not spend) much money.
David (8) _____ (rain) much?
Sara No, the sun (9) _____ (shine) most days.
David (10) _____ (have) any problems?
Sara Well, I (11) _____ (fall) off my bike once, and we (12) _____ (forget) to bring Band-Aids, but we (13) _____ (not have) any mechanical problems!
David What (14) _____ (do) in the evenings?
Sara We (15) _____ (find) a campsite, and then we (16) _____ (go) shopping in the nearest town, (17) _____ (cook) a big dinner, (18) _____ (eat) lots of food, and (19) _____ (drink) wine. It (20) _____ (be) great!
David When (21) _____ (get back)?
Sara I (22) _____ (fly) home last Sunday, but my friends (23) _____ (come) back three days later. They (24) _____ (not want) to leave Arizona!

2 Short answers

Answer the following questions about Sara's vacation. Use short answers.

1. "Did she go to Arizona?" "*Yes, she did*   ."
2. "Did they camp every night?"
   "_____."
3. "Did Sara have an accident?"
   "_____."
4. "Did they all come home at the same time?"
   "_____."
5. "Was it expensive to camp?"
   "_____."
6. "Was the weather good most of the time?"
   "_____."

Past Continuous

1 Forming the Past Continuous

What were these people doing at 6 o'clock yesterday evening? Make sentences using the Past Continuous.

1. John / not listen to the radio / watch television
   John wasn't listening to the radio.
   He was watching television.

2. Maria / not work / drive home
   _____
   _____

3. We / not swim / sit in a traffic jam
   _____
   _____

4. Matthew and Peter / not run / play tennis
   _____
   _____

5. I / not watch a movie / take a bath
   _____
   _____

6. Justin / not read / cook dinner
   _____
   _____

2 *What were you doing?*

Answer the following questions about you.

What were you doing at . . .

1. 6:00 yesterday morning?
   _____

2. 8:00 A.M. yesterday?
   _____

3. 10:00 P.M. last Sunday?
   _____

4. noon yesterday?
   _____

5. 5:30 P.M. the day before yesterday?
   _____

6. 2:30 yesterday afternoon?
   _____

3 Past Simple or Continuous?

Put the verb in parentheses in the Past Simple or the Past Continuous.

Last week I *decided* (decide) to invite some friends over for dinner. I (1) _____ (buy) lots of delicious food, including some imported ham. At about 6:00 I (2) _____ (cook) in the kitchen. The sun (3) _____ (shine) and it (4) _____ (be) a beautiful evening, so I (5) _____ (open) the back door. Then the telephone (6) _____ (ring). I (7) _____ (go) to answer it, and when I (8) _____ (come) back the ham (9) _____ (not be) on the table. I (10) _____ (look) out of the window. A cat (11) _____ (sit) in my yard on a wall, and it (12) _____ (eat) my ham. What (13) _____ (can) I do? I (14) _____ (fill) a pan with water and (15) _____ (go) quietly outside. The cat (16) _____ (not look) in my direction, and it (17) _____ (enjoy) the ham so much that it (18) _____ (not hear) me. I (19) _____ (walk) slowly up to it—I (20) _____ (want) to empty the water over its head. A little cruel, I know, but the ham (21) _____ (be) very expensive! But at the last minute the cat (22) _____ (hear) me, (23) _____ (jump) over the wall, and (24) _____ (escape). The happiest cat in the neighborhood . . .

Verb patterns 1

1 *Would you like* or *do you like*?

1 Complete the following questions using *would you like* or *do you like*.

   1. *Do you like* walking?
   2. _____ to go to the movies?
   3. _____ going to the movies?
   4. What _____ to drink?
   5. _____ to go for a walk?
   6. What drinks _____?

2 Match the questions and answers.

   a. ___ Mineral water, please.
   b. ___ Usually, but I hate horror movies.
   c. *1* Yes, especially in the mountains.
   d. ___ Yes, it's beautiful weather.
   e. ___ It depends what's on.
   f. ___ Ice tea and soda.

2 Infinitive or -ing?

Put the verb in parentheses in the correct form, infinitive or -ing. Sometimes both are possible.

1. I want _to sell_ (sell) my car.
2. I'm thinking of _____ (buy) a car.
3. She hopes _____ (be) here by 7:00.
4. I love _____ (watch) black and white movies.
5. I'd like _____ (continue) _____ (study), but I haven't got enough money.
6. We finished _____ (paint) the house last week.
7. Would you like _____ (work) in a hospital?
8. He started _____ (play) golf last year.
9. I've decided _____ (train) to be an occupational therapist.

will and going to

Choosing the correct form

Underline the correct verb form in the following sentences.

1. "I'm cold."
   "*I'll put*/*I'm going to put* the heat on."
2. "Can I speak to Marco?"
   "Hold on, *I'll get*/*I'm going to get* him."
3. "Coffee or tea?"
   "*I'll have*/*I'm going to have* tea, please."
4. "Has Mike got any plans for the weekend?"
   "Yes, *he'll visit*/*he's going to visit* his grandparents."
5. "Cathy's on the phone for you."
   "Can she call back? *I'll take*/*I'm going to take* a bath."
6. "*I'll go*/*I'm going to go* to the supermarket."
   "Oh, *will you*/*are you*? I think *I'll come*/*I'm going to come* with you."
7. "Did you get my fax?"
   "No, I didn't."
   "OK, *I'll send*/*I'm going to send* it again."
8. "Sophie? *Will you marry me*/*Are you going to marry me*?"
   "Oh, James! Yes, of course, *I will*/*I'm going to*."

Present Perfect

1 Making affirmative and negative sentences

Have you ever done these things? Put ✓ or ✗ next to each one. Then write sentences.

write a letter to a newspaper   ✗
ski in Utah
meet a famous person
visit the White House
win a prize
sing in public
read Hemingway's *The Sun Also Rises*

1. _I've never written a letter to a newspaper._
2. _____
3. _____
4. _____
5. _____
6. _____
7. _____

2 Making questions

Put the words in the correct order to ask a question, and write true answers.

1. ever/you/to/Australia/been/have
   Have you ever been to Australia ?   _Yes, I have._
2. haircut/you/have/a/had/recently
   _____ ?
3. year/have/movies/this/you/seen/what
   _____ ?
4. ever/cigarette/a/you/smoked/have
   _____ ?
5. restaurant/eaten/a/you/have/in/week/this
   _____ ?
6. any/you/have/CDs/bought/month/this
   _____ ?

3 Present Perfect or Past Simple?

Put the verb in parentheses in the Present Perfect or the Past Simple.

Interviewer Today I'm talking to Tony Crooks, the American movie director. Tell me, Tony, how long *have you been* (be) a movie director?

Tony Well, I (1) _____ (study) movie-making in college in the 1970s, and I (2) _____ (work) as a director for over 20 years now.

Interviewer What (3) _____ (be) the first movie you (4) _____ (make)?

Tony *A Prisoner's Life* in 1978, but I (5) _____ (lose) the only copy a year later so nobody (6) _____ (see) it since then! My first successful movie (7) _____ (be) *Always*, which (8) _____ (come out) in 1982.

Interviewer And how many countries (9) _____ (visit)? (10) _____ (make) movies outside the United States?

Tony I (11) _____ (not work) in many countries—only the United States, Germany, and Australia. Last month I (12) _____ (fly) to Montreal and (13) _____ (spend) two weeks filming there.

Interviewer When (14) _____ (go) to Australia?

Tony In 1995. I (15) _____ (want) to make a TV documentary called *The Outback*, about life in rural areas, and I (16) _____ (drive) all the way from Sydney to Perth.

Interviewer What are the best things about your job?

Tony The travel and the people. I (17) _____ (travel) all over the world, going to film festivals and so on. And I (18) _____ (meet) some great people.

Interviewer (19) _____ (start) any new projects recently?

Tony Yes, last week I (20) _____ (sign) a contract for a new movie set in China.

Interviewer Well, thank you, Tony—it (21) _____ (be) very interesting talking to you …